Looking at Life Cycles

Butterfly

Victoria Huseby

A+

Smart Apple Media

Smart Apple Media is published by Black Rabbit Books
P.O. Box 3263, Mankato, Minnesota 56002

Printed in the United States

Published by arrangement with the Watts Publishing Group Ltd, London.

Editor: Rachel Tonkin
Designer: Chris Fraser
Illustrator: John Alston
Picture researcher: Diana Morris
Science consultant: Andrew Solway
Literacy consultant: Gill Matthews

Picture Credits:
Stephen Dalton/NHPA: 21; John Fowler/Photographers Direct: 5, 17;
Robert Pickett/Ecoscene: 13, 15; Glenn M. Richardson: 7, 9, 11;
Colin Tracy/Photographers Direct: front cover, 1, 19

Library of Congress Cataloging-in-Publication Data

Huseby, Victoria.
    Butterfly / by Victoria Huseby.
      p. cm.–(Smart Apple Media. Looking at life cycles)
      Summary: "An introduction to the life cycle of a butterfly from egg to adult"–Provided by
publisher.
      Includes index.
      ISBN 978-1-59920-174-0
      1. Butterflies–Life cycles–Juvenile literature. I. Title.
QL544.2.H88 2009
595.78'9–dc22
                                                                                    2007030462

9 8 7 6 5 4 3 2 1

Contents

Laying Eggs

A butterfly is an **insect**.
An insect has six legs
and **antennae**, or feelers,
on its head. In spring,
a female butterfly lays
her eggs on leaves.

Inside the Egg

The butterfly's eggs stick to the leaves. Inside each egg, a **caterpillar** is growing. It takes 10 days for the caterpillar to grow.

New Caterpillar

A caterpillar hatches from the egg. The caterpillar eats leaves to help it grow. It makes a **leaf tent** to live in. It uses special silk to stick the leaves together.

Shedding Skin

After a few days, the
caterpillar sheds its skin
so that it can grow bigger.
The caterpillar wraps itself
in leaves again while it
grows a new skin.

Fully Grown

When a caterpillar is fully grown, it is ready to turn into a butterfly. It hangs from a leaf stem.

Pupa

The caterpillar sheds its skin
again to form a **pupa**.
This takes a few hours.
The pupa is covered in a
chrysalis. This keeps it safe.

Changing

Inside the chrysalis, the pupa
changes into a butterfly.
After about three weeks,
the chrysalis splits open.
A butterfly crawls out.

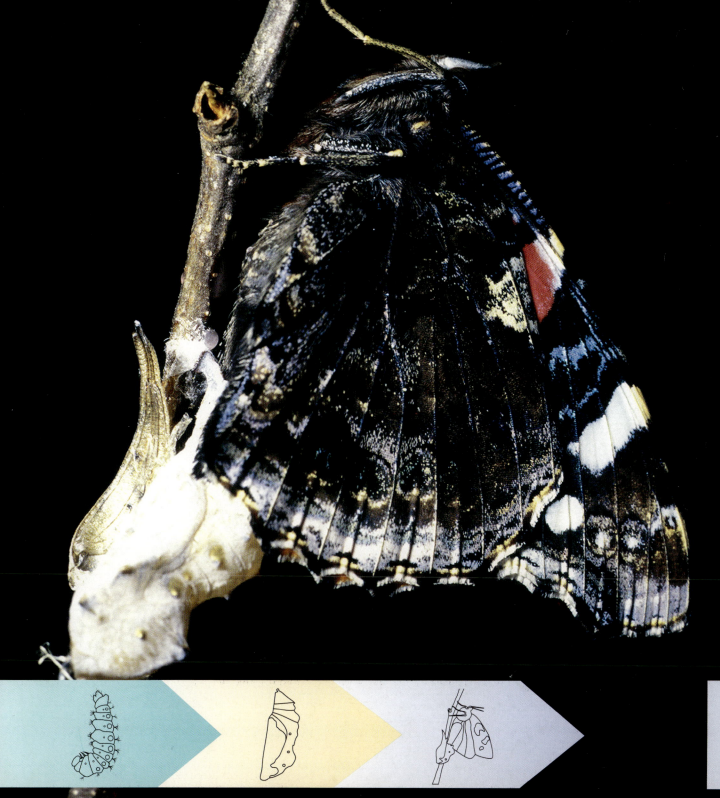

New Butterfly

The new butterfly's wings
are wrinkled. It climbs up
the plant to shake out its
wings. Then it flies away.

   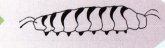

Flying Away

In fall, some butterflies **migrate**. They fly to warmer places. The butterflies come back in spring to lay their eggs on leaves.

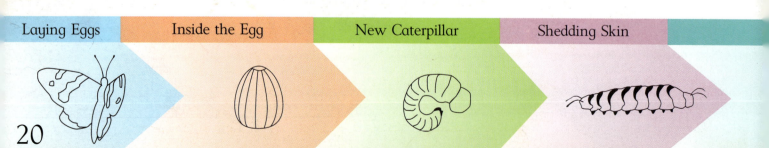

| Laying Eggs | Inside the Egg | New Caterpillar | Shedding Skin |

Fully Grown	Pupa	Changing	New Butterfly

21

Butterfly Facts

- The color and shape of a butterfly's eggs are different for each type of butterfly.

- Some butterflies live for only three days. Others can live for six months.

- Some butterflies can be as big as 12 inches (30 cm) wide.

- Some butterflies fly thousands of miles when they migrate.

- Butterflies have small hairs on their feet. When they stand on food, they can taste it.

- A butterfly's tongue is like a drinking straw so that it can sip nectar from flowers. When it is not eating, its tongue curls up out of the way.

- Butterflies' wings are covered with lots of tiny scales. This is what gives them their color.

Glossary

Antennae
The feelers on the head of an insect. They are used for smelling.

Caterpillar
The stage in the life of a butterfly between hatching from an egg and forming a pupa.

Chrysalis
A hard outer shell that protects the pupa inside as it changes into a butterfly.

Insect
An animal with six legs and two antennae. The body of an insect is divided into three parts.

Leaf tent
A covering of folded leaves that protects caterpillars while they grow.

Migrate
To fly from one place to another at regular times of the year.

Pupa
The third stage in the life of a butterfly, between being a caterpillar and becoming an adult butterfly.

23

Index and Web Sites

For Kids:

Butterfly Life Cycle
http://www.tooter4kids.com/LifeCycle/Butterfly_Life_Cycle.htm

Butterfly Life Cycle Printout
http://www.enchantedlearning.com/subjects/butterfly/activities/printouts/lifecycle.shtml

Where Do Butterflies Come From?
http://www.hhmi.org/coolscience/butterfly/index.html

For Teachers:

A to Z Teacher Stuff: Life Cycles
http://atozteacherstuff.com/Themes/Life_Cycles/

Butterfly Curricula—The Butterfly Web Site
http://butterflywebsite.com/educate/index.cfm